To Market, To Market
by Donna Foley

PEARSON

Scott
Foresman

Editorial Offices: Glenview, Illinois • Parsippany, New Jersey • New York, New York
Sales Offices: Needham, Massachusetts • Duluth, Georgia • Glenview, Illinois
Coppell, Texas • Sacramento, California • Mesa, Arizona

Crops of fruits and vegetables might grow where you live.
In the summer you can buy fruits and vegetables at a farmer's market.

In the winter there may not be a farmer's market.

It is too cold for crops to grow in some places during the winter.

Grocery stores also sell fruits and vegetables. Farmers, or **producers**, from warmer places grow food that is sold to stores in colder places.

Consumers can find many kinds of food at the grocery store.
Foods that do not grow near you are sent to your grocery store all year.

Some foods may be sent to you as a present. You might get mangoes from Mexico and peaches or pecans from South Carolina.

You and your family can enjoy food from near and far.

Glossary

consumer someone who buys and uses goods

crop a kind of plant that people grow and use

producer someone who makes or grows something